Trading

Day Trading: for Beginners: The Day Trading Guide for Making Money with Stocks, Options, Forex and More + A Comprehensive Guide to Making Money with Day Trading

© **Copyright 2017**

All rights Reserved. No part of this book may be reproduced in any form without permission in writing from the author. Reviewers may quote brief passages in reviews.

Disclaimer

No part of this publication may be reproduced or transmitted in any form or by any means, mechanical or electronic, including photocopying or recording, or by any information storage and retrieval system, or transmitted by email without permission in writing from the publisher.

While all attempts have been made to verify the information provided in this publication, neither the author nor the publisher assumes any responsibility for errors, omissions or contrary interpretations of the subject matter herein.

This book is for entertainment purposes only. The views expressed are those of the author alone, and should not be taken as expert instruction or commands. The reader is responsible for his or her own actions.

Adherence to all applicable laws and regulations, including international, federal, state and local laws governing professional licensing, business practices, advertising and all other aspects of doing business in the US, Canada, UK or any other jurisdiction is the sole responsibility of the purchaser or reader.

Neither the author nor the publisher assumes any responsibility or liability whatsoever on the behalf of the purchaser or reader of these materials. Any perceived slight of any individual or organization is purely unintentional.

Contents

BOOK 1: DAY TRADING FOR BEGINNERS 1

INTRODUCTION... 2

1. IS DAY TRADING RIGHT FOR YOU? 3

2. WHAT DO YOU NEED TO BE A DAY TRADER? 6

3. HOW TO SET UP A BROKERAGE ACCOUNT 8

4. SOME THINGS TO KNOW FIRST 11

5. TRADING PATTERNS AND STRATEGIES..............15

    NEWS TRADING 16

    TRENDING 18

    SCALPING 19

    CONTRARIAN TRADING 19

    INTUITIVE TRADING... 21

    PRICE ACTION TRADING 24

    CHANNEL OR RANGE TRADING... 26

    FIBONACCI RATIOS 27

6. TRADING ON MARGIN 31

7. DAY TRADING IN OPTIONS 33

    OPTIONS TERMINOLOGY 37

    THE "COVERED CALL": A CONSERVATIVE STRATEGY........ 38

    IS OPTIONS TRADING FOR YOU? 42

8. DAY TRADING ON THE FOREIGN EXCHANGE MARKET 44

- THE FOREIGN EXCHANGE MARKET 46
- WHY EXCHANGE RATES VARY 49
- DAY TRADING FOREX 50

CONCLUSION 51
BOOK 2: DAY TRADING 53
PREFACE 54
CHAPTER 1 INTRODUCTION TO DAY TRADING 56
CHAPTER 2 TECHNICAL ANALYSIS 70
CHAPTER 3 TRADING STRATEGIES AND SIGNALS 76
CHAPTER 4 CASE STUDY OF SONNY ELIAS 88
CHAPTER 5 MARYELLEN CURTIS CASE 95
CHAPTER 6 LAURA DAHL CASE 104
CHAPTER 7 PARTIAL LIST OF DAY TRADING BROKERS 108
CONCLUSION 110

Book 1: Day Trading for Beginners
The Day Trading Guide for Making Money with Stocks, Options, Forex and More

Introduction

I want to thank you and commend you for downloading the book, "Day Trading: The Day Trading Guide for Making Money with Stocks, Options, Forex and More."

This book will introduce you to day trading, starting with the important question, is it right for you? If it is, this book will tell you how to get started, how to make money, how to avoid losing money, and a lot of the technical information you'll need.

Thanks again for downloading this book, I hope you enjoy it!

1. Is Day Trading Right for You?

When J.P. Morgan was asked what the market would
do that day, he said, "It will fluctuate."

"Day trading" means buying and selling stocks so that you close out all trades at the end of the day. When the market closes in the evening, you no longer own any of the stocks you've been trading, and hopefully, you've made some money on your trades. With discipline and knowledge, you can make quite a bit of money day trading – and enjoy doing it, too.

You need to understand that day trading is not investment. It is also not gambling. It's speculation, and here's the difference: a roulette wheel at the casino is purely random. Even if you don't know the exact odds on every kind of bet, you can be sure that the casino does. A few people will make a lot of money and most people (except for the ones who own the casino!) will lose money, and it's completely unpredictable which group is which. On the other hand, putting money into a bank savings account is as close to a sure deal as you will ever get in this uncertain world. It's also a rock-solid certainty that you won't make very much money that way.

Investing in the stock market means studying individual companies to determine their real value, and putting money into those that have a good future ahead. If you do this conscientiously, you will almost certainly make money... but there's a bit of randomness in this, and sometimes all the care you can give won't be enough to avoid losing some money.

Playing poker follows this rule: you can't win without both luck and skill, but you can always lose by playing badly. That is, the hand that a poker player draws is determined by pure luck, but what he does with his luck depends on skill.

Day trading has more risk than investing, but also can yield better returns. It depends less on luck than poker, usually pays better, and you don't have to keep that stiff "poker face"!

If the charts only contain random wavy lines, then day trading would be gambling. If you knew exactly where the price of a stock was going, it would be a sure thing (hint: forget it!).

The fluctuations in daily stock prices are almost-but-not-quite random, and it's that little edge of predictability that will allow you to make a profit in day trading. No day trader makes a profit every day, but with knowledge and discipline, you can come out ahead often, better than most people can do by investing and much more controllable than gambling.

2. What Do You Need to Be a Day Trader?

First and most importantly, you need to be the kind of person who can learn from study, who can make decisions based on rational thinking and not emotions, who can make a plan and follow it, who can lose money without getting upset and make money without getting giddy, and who has at least a couple of hours in the mornings and in the afternoons which can be devoted to day trading with no interruptions.

Next, you need some money you can afford to lose. If you can't afford to lose any money, or you get anxious whenever you do, this activity is not for you.

You need a direct electronic account with a brokerage that offers support for day traders (see the next section).

You should have a fairly new computer with a reliable, fast Internet connection. Here's a tip: if you are using a laptop on your home wi-fi, run a cable from the router directly to your computer's ethernet port and connect that way instead. It will be faster and more secure. Trying to trade on a non-secured wi-fi network is just asking for trouble, so don't try to pursue this career at the coffee shop. It's very handy to add a second monitor if your computer will support this.

Finally, you need time to learn and study before you launch into day trading. Spend enough time doing fictional, practice trades that you can be confident of your decisions before you trade for real.

3. How to Set Up a Brokerage Account

As a day trader, you will need an on-line trading account so that you can execute your own trades. Traditional brokerages let you call your broker, get advice from him or her, and buy or sell stocks. This is often extremely helpful. But a day trader might be executing orders every few minutes, which your broker can't handle, and you also must get the lower fees associated with doing your own trades, or you won't make a profit.

Here's a good list of brokerages that will set up a day-trading account for you:

https://www.nerdwallet.com/blog/investing/best-online-brokers-for-stock-trading/

Here's what you should look for in choosing a brokerage:

- Price. Since you will be trading all the time, you need a low price for each trade. But be cautious here: brokers have, to use some technical terminology, a whole boatload of ways to charge you money, and a broker with low per-trade fees might turn out to be very expensive. Fees can include account maintenance fees, account inactivity fees, charges for telephone calls, and even more creative tricks.

- Minimum starting balance. You need to put some money into the account, and be prepared to say goodbye to it. That is (to repeat): don't put any money into a brokerage account that you can't afford to lose.

- Trading platform. This means the software you will use for trading, which might be an application you download to your computer (in which case, be sure it runs on your system), or a program that runs on the brokerage's server, which you will reach using your internet browser. Try this software out before making a commitment. If it seems confusing or slow, you may want to shop around for another brokerage.

- Brokerage services. A brokerage that is set up for traditional investors can provide invaluable research about stocks. As a day trader, you're not looking for the same qualities as a long-term investor, but if you don't mind paying for the information, it can still be very useful to you.

4. Some Things to Know First

We'll start out, in this book, discussing day trading in the stock market. Other markets are also good for day trading, and are discussed later.

A **candlestick graph** represents the price changes to a stock over some period of time, which might be a day, an hour or part of an hour. This technique, interestingly enough, was actually developed in the 18th century in Japan to describe the price of rice, which explains the Japanese terminology.

This book will discuss stock prices by talking about the candlestick graph because it's a very common graph type, and conveys quite a bit of useful information. On a candlestick graph, the lines at the top and bottom (which are called "shadows") mark off the highest and lowest prices for that stock during the period covered (which might be as short as a minute). The candle body is dark if the price is going down - that is, if the closing price was less than the opening price. The body is light if the price is going up. If the stock comes back to about the same place it started, you get a cross called a "doji". If the price didn't move at all, the candlestick graph is just a horizontal line with no shadows.

A **long sale** is what you probably think of as normal: you buy stock when the price is low and you expect it to go up. If it does, you sell the stock at a profit. A **short sale** is a way to make money if you expect the price to go down. In a short sale, the broker loans you some shares of stock so that you can sell them, even though you don't own them. During the day, you'll have to buy enough shares to pay back the broker. If the price does go down, then you can buy the shares for less than you sold them for, and you make a profit. If the price goes up, you made the wrong decision. You still have to buy that stock to give it back to the broker, but now you'll have to pay even more for it.

Using both techniques, a day trader who makes correct predictions can profit from any movement in price, up or down.

A **stop-loss order** is a vital tool you must use to limit the amount you can lose on a bad purchase of stock. You set a stop-loss for whatever amount of loss you can tolerate, based on the price of the stock or a percentage change. If the stock price goes down below the stop-loss price, your broker will sell it automatically. No one likes to lose money, but a stop-loss will protect you from losing more than you want to. The stop-loss point is not a mathematical decision, it's based on your financial situation and your personality: it represents how much you are willing to lose before you call it quits.

Liquidity means how easily you can buy or sell a stock. An "illiquid" stock has only a few people trading it, which can be a problem: you can't buy if no one is selling or sell if no one is buying. For day trading, you want highly liquid stocks.

Volatility refers to how much the stock price moves up or down in a day. If the price doesn't move much, a day trader can't make money on it. On the other hand, a stock with too much volatility (that is, the price swings wildly) probably means that a lot of traders are reacting to rumors or irrational fears, and a careful day trader will want to stay out of that market.

Slippage is the amount of price movement that happens between the time you place an order and the time the order is executed. Slippage is always bad and you want to minimize it. It depends on the kind of trading software you use, the speed of your internet connection, the volatility of the stock, the current load on your broker, and the overall activity level of the market.

5. Trading Patterns and Strategies

When you study a stock price's daily movements long enough, you will see patterns that emerge, and strategies for buying and selling that would be profitable. This list describes some of the patterns that day traders look for, and strategies they use.

The interesting thing about these patterns is that every one of them works... some of the time. Every one of them will also fail, some of the time. If there were a guaranteed strategy that always worked, of course everybody would use it. But nothing in the world actually works that way, and it's emphatically not true for day trading.

Here's what does work: every day trader develops his own strategy, using a mixture of patterns that are unique. No two day traders will operate exactly the same way. This means, first, that you can come up with a strategy that will work for you, and second, that you (like every day trader) will be a pioneer trying something that no one else has done. That's part of what makes it fun!

One last caveat, which is so obvious that it's easy to overlook: if you think it's the right time to buy stock, necessarily somebody else thinks it's the right time to sell. You can't sell stock unless somebody else wants to buy it. In every transaction, one side is right and the other side is wrong. Your edge is your experience, your constant attention, and your disciplined adherence to a strategy.

News Trading

The stock market is twitchy about news. Every financial story that appears on TV, and many of the non-financial news stories, will send some stocks up and some down. For example, you hear that a pipeline has burst in Kansas. This is obviously bad news for the pipeline company, for the oil companies that ship on that pipeline, for any business in a town that might be affected by the physical oil, for wheat farmers whose crops may be spoiled, for food companies that buy wheat or for any oil company that has a pending application to build a pipeline anywhere else in America. It's good news for spill-remediation companies or food companies that use some other grain. It might be good or bad for truckers, who might get tanker business while the pipeline is being repaired, but who also might have to pay higher gas prices. It might be good or bad for organic-food companies, pipeline control and instrumentation companies, or alternative energy companies.

How can you tell which stocks will rise and which will fall? You need experience and expertise in some particular sub-set of the market. No one can keep track of all of the effects of a news story, but you can get an edge by understanding one little corner of the market.

It's important to understand that as a day trader, you really aren't concerned with what a news story *actually* means for companies. Because you are trading on a time horizon of hours or less, you are only trying to gauge the immediate reactions of other traders and investors. You are trying to anticipate how *they* will feel about this story. In other words, this is a problem in psychology more than a problem in economics.

You will need to keep a continuous eye on news from multiple sources to use this strategy. Professional traders tend to work in a sea of monitors showing financial and business news from sources such as CNN or Bloomberg.

Trending

Trending is also called momentum trading. This the simplest pattern, and simplicity can be a good thing! It just means seeing which way the price seems to be going, and assuming it will keep going that way for a while. The reason you make this assumption is that you've watched this stock, and noticed that that's the way the price seems to move.

Trend day trading is about watching the price graph, not about second-guessing why a stock is moving or who is buying and selling. Your goal here is to identify when a stock starts moving in one direction, based on similar movements you've watched in the past. Any trend movement will stop and reverse after a while, and it's up to you to have a sense of when that will be so that you can get out on time.

Don't neglect to have a stop-loss order on every stock you trade by trends.

Scalping

A "scalper" makes money by executing a lot of very quick, very small trades. He buys a stock and sells it, often only a few minutes later, when it has gone up a few cents. He shorts a stock and buys when the price has gone down a few cents.

Repeat this pattern a hundred or more times in a day, and you can make a good total profit by the end of the day. (This strategy depends crucially on getting a very cheap price for each trade from your broker.) Because you need to buy and sell fairly large blocks of stock to make a significant profit, however, this strategy increases your risk of loss.

Contrarian Trading

Sarah Palin had a scornful proverb for those who follow trends: "Only dead fish go with the flow." Stocks always go up after a down-trend and down after an up-trend. Clearly, if you bet against the trend, you're bound to be right some of the time, and you get the satisfaction of telling yourself you're not just part of the crowd.

However, you don't need to be very smart just to see which way the parade is going and march the other way. A successful contrarian doesn't need or make use of an opinion on which way the whole market is going. Instead, a contrarian looks for an unloved stock that, for some irrational reason, is trading below its true value, or for a stock that has been over-hyped so that it is priced higher than the company is really worth. In either situation, the trend is bound to reverse, and the contrarian wants to get there before everybody else figures this out.

A day-trading contrarian faces a slightly different problem. Since you want to close out all transactions before the end of the day, you will need to look for irrational price movements that go up and down within hours.

Sometimes this happens because of news. Example: X Company announces a management reorganization, and the stock price goes down. You get your advantage by knowing something about X Company. If you think that other investors are just being hysterical and the management re-org was needed and will make the company stronger, then you should watch the price go down until the stock is clearly undervalued, then buy. If the market comes to its senses before the end of the day, the price will go back up by the time you sell.

An opposite example: Y Drugs announces tests of a new drug to cure Creeping Crud (or something). The market goes crazy and the price spikes. By understanding the news better than most, you know that Y Drugs is several years away from having a marketable product, so you short the stock when it is high enough to be clearly overvalued.

Sometimes an irrational price can occur because of movements of the whole market – that is, the Dow Jones average (or some other collective indicator of your choice) goes up or down, and takes stocks with it that are really not affected by whatever elation or depression has caused the investors to move. If you believe the correction will come during the day for those particular stocks, you can place a contrary order and make a profit.

Intuitive Trading

Here's a swell fifty-cent word for you: *pareidolia* (par-i-DOL-ee-ah). It's the reason why people see faces in things that don't actually have faces, such as the "Man in the Moon", the tail ends of cars, or toast with splotchy burns. It means the human tendency to want to make meaningful patterns out of the data we see, even if the data is random.

This is also the reason why every slot-machine player in Las Vegas has a theory that predicts when a slot machine is going to pay off, such as "after you've lost twenty times in a row" or "when you get two cherries with another cherry only one space away" or "in the early morning when not many people are playing". Of course all of these theories are worthless, since slot machines pay off at random.

But pareidolia is related to the deeply human ability to extract *real* patterns when they aren't obvious. People are much better at doing this than computers, because it's an evolutionary skill that was important to our distant ancestors.

For example, if you watch a lot of movies, you may have the ability to look at a character in the first ten minutes and say, "That guy's going to get killed before the end." You can do this even if you can't say why you think that, because your brain is processing many subtle signals that are below the level of consciousness.

An "intuitive" day-trader can develop a gut-instinct about how the market will move, after a learning period that might require years. If you have this ability, it's quite legitimate to use it in trading, and can be very profitable. Intuitive traders often say they are following a strategy even when they really aren't, because they're afraid they will look silly if they say they're following a hunch.

However, this is an extremely tricky strategy and it's very easy to fool yourself – and lose a lot of money! A valid hunch is different from an emotional reaction, or the desire to follow the crowd or to go the other way from the crowd, or the desire to look smarter than you are, or dozens of other psychological tricks your brain can play on you.

A good intuitive trader absorbs vast amounts of information, studies the price charts and avoids committing to "theories" that aren't real. Instead, an intuitive trader tests his gut instinct against data. If your hunches tend to be good, it's okay to follow them.

But if you (like most people) are not naturally and correctly intuitive, you should develop a strategy and stick to it, without making sudden impulsive buys or sales.

Price Action Trading

A "price-action" trader looks at short-term candlestick patterns rather than the overall movement of a stock price.

The harami pattern involves two candlesticks next to each other, of different colors. The first has a long body, and the second has a short body entirely within the limits of the longer body.

What the **harami** means, to a price-action trader, is that a trend has just run out its course and is starting to reverse. If the first, longer candlestick is black (meaning prices are going down, pretty fast) and the next candlestick is white (meaning prices are going up, but tentatively), that indicates that the down-trend may be over.

If the opposite occurs, and the first candlestick indicates an up-trend and the second indicates a tentative downward movement, then the up-trend may be about to change.

The harami is particularly significant if the two

candlesticks represent the closing price one day and the opening price the next day.

The **harami-cross** pattern is the same as the harami, except that the second candlestick is a doji or cross, which indicates that the price movement of the first candlestick has stopped, and now the price is hardly moving at all. The harami-cross pattern is a stronger version of the harami, which indicates that the previous price movement has completely "run out of steam". This probably means the direction is about to reverse.

Engulfing is a pattern that means sentiment about a stock has just shifted abruptly. The picture shows the engulfing pattern between the close of trading one day and the opening the next morning.

The bearish engulfing tells this story: the stock was going up yesterday at the close, and this morning's opening price was up even higher. But then the price went down so far that it closed well below yesterday's lowest price. This means that the "bears" feel pretty strongly that the stock was overvalued, and the price is likely to go down even more.

The bullish engulfing is the opposite story. Even though this stock was going down yesterday, and today opened even lower, some traders believe so much in this stock that they have driven the price above yesterday's best. If they believe the stock is worth more, other traders probably will also, and the price will keep going up.

The **dragonfly** doji (you can see the Japanese influence here!) is a cross doji with a long lower shadow and little or no top shadow. It tells this story: the bears tried to push the price down but were ultimately unsuccessful, because the open, high and close prices are all the same. This may tell you (if confirmed by your other information) that there is quite a bit of support for this stock and the price is likely to go up.

The **gravestone** doji is just the opposite.

Channel or Range Trading

You've probably noticed in your own life that some prices bring emotional reactions. If you're going out to lunch, $12 seems way too high (even though paying that much for supper doesn't seem unreasonable), but lunch for $4 makes you think the food's probably terrible. (Your particular inflection points will vary, of course.)

Many stocks seem to have emotional barriers at the

high end (meaning that many traders get the idea the stock has gone too high) and the low end. You can identify this pattern by looking for sharp reversals in the price line, with a repeating pattern over several days.

A channel trader buys when the price goes below the "channel" (often by setting an automatic "buy" order) and sells when the price goes back up. In the same way, a channel trader sells short when the price goes above the channel.

Fibonacci Ratios

This trading pattern is range trading with some special numbers.

If you're the kind of person who thinks math is fun (which is a good mental habit for traders), then you've no doubt met the Fibonacci numbers, a remarkable sequence that mathematicians always enjoy. If you haven't met them, try:

https://www.mathsisfun.com/numbers/ fibonacci-sequence.html, but note that you don't really need to know all this stuff for the purpose of trading.

What you will be concerned with as a trader is several "magic" ratios. We won't explain here where these numbers come from, but you will need to be familiar with these ratios:

$$61.8\%, 38.2\%, 23.6\%$$

There are two reasons why the Fibonacci ratios are important. First, they show up over and over again in nature. These ratios are found in the spiral shells of snails, in the arrangement of flower petals around the center, in population growth, in probability theory, in pine cones – for whatever reason, the Fibonacci ratios are deeply embedded in the living and non-living world.

More directly related to trading, the Fibonacci ratios also seem to be baked into the human soul. The "Golden Ratio" is 0.618 to 1, and rectangles of this shape have been used by architects and artists for thousands of years. The Parthenon in Greece is famously based on the Golden Ratio, with the same ratio controlling the overall width and height of the building, the relationship between the ground and the lintel, and the lintel and the roof ... and many more. Researchers have tried showing pictures of various buildings and shapes to people who have never heard of the Fibonacci ratios, and consistently, people say that shapes based on that ratio "just look nicer" than shapes that are not. For some reason, people appear to be born with a feeling for the Fibonacci ratios.

And by the way, handsome men and pretty women tend to have ratios between their facial features, such as the distance from mouth to eyes and mouth to nose, that are about that 61.8% point. Hope that's you! (If not, you should learn day trading and make a lot of money, which makes anybody more attractive, right?)

Another study found that people tend to get anxious or sad when they spend more than 61.8% of the money in their wallets. This leads directly to the theory of Fibonacci ratios in trading:

People tend to have an emotional reaction when prices, after a trend, move to positions that correspond to the Fibonacci ratios.

If this sounds flaky to you, consider that while it may not be real, the market is full of traders who have read books like this, and *they* think it's real, which means that this is something of a self-fulfilling prophecy.

This theory is so common that trading-graphics

software often includes a tool to draw the Fibonacci ratios automatically.

6. Trading on Margin

"Margin" is the term traders use for borrowing money to make trades. The amount of margin a trader can get depends on the amount of money he has in his brokerage account, and also on his history with that broker.

A trader with margin can buy stock with, say, 30% of his own money and 70% borrowed from the broker, which lets him buy and sell much larger blocks of stock than he could do on his own. If he trades successfully, he makes that much more money on each share. He can pay back the broker and keep a larger profit, often many hundreds of times larger.

Here's the rule on margin trading:

Many day traders can make more money by trading on margin.

However, not you.

Yes, seriously.

The reason why you can't successfully trade on margin is because you are reading this book, which is aimed at introducing beginners to the world of day trading. If you knew enough about trading to handle a margin account, you wouldn't be here.

Margin trading offers much higher rewards at a much higher risk. You can make or lose fortunes in the course of a single day. Debt is often called "leverage" because you use only a small amount of your own money to swing very large trades. Here's what you need to know about leverage: leverage let's you control a big swing with a small effort. But of course, it works both ways!

So the rule is, when you have enough experience to be able to trade with leverage (and probably long after you've forgotten about reading this not-really-joking joke), your broker will offer you a margin account. Until then, it's not for you.

7. Day Trading in Options

Like many things, you have to buy an "option" for money. What you have bought is a contract that gives you the right to either buy some stock at a fixed price within a time limit (a "call") or the right to sell some stock at a fixed price within a time limit (a "put").

You can either buy or sell options.

An option is optional for you, as the buyer - you don't have to use it if you don't want to. This saves you from having to do a trade that will cost you money, but then you will have spent the price you paid for the option for nothing.

But when you are the buyer, an option is not at all

optional for the seller. If you have bought the right to buy stock at the set price, the seller *must* sell it to you at that price, even if he doesn't want to – and of course he would prefer not to sell, because the only reason you want to buy that stock is that it's worth more now than you will pay. If you have bought the right to sell stock, the buyer *has* to buy it even though the only reason you're selling is because the price has gone down and you can sell it for more.

Here's a table that summarizes how options work for the buyer:

You bought a ...	Price Rises	Price Falls	Option Expires
PUT option	You would be sad if you had to exercise this option, because you'd have to sell the stock at the agreed price, even though it's selling for more now. Fortunately, you don't have to do this.	*You're happy!* You get to sell a block of stock at the agreed price, but you can buy it right now for less than that, so you make money on the difference.	*You're annoyed but also relieved.* You bought an option you didn't use, so you wasted the price of the option. On the other hand, you didn't lose any more than that.
CALL option	*You're happy!* You can buy the stock at the agreed price, which is less than the current price. You could sell that stock immediately, and make money on the difference.	You would be sad if you had to exercise this option, because you'd have to buy the stock for the agreed price even though it's not worth that much now. Fortunately, you don't have to do this.	

You can be a buyer or seller of put options, or a

buyer or seller of call options. If you buy an option, some other trader sold it to you. One of you thinks the price will go up, the other thinks the price will go down. Obviously, you can't both be right.

If you decide not to exercise an option you buy (because you'd lose money on the deal), you do nothing, and the option time expires. In this case, the seller makes a little money because he keeps the option price, and you lose the same amount.

Options are what is called a zero-sum game: if the buyer makes money, the seller loses money, and vice-versa. Options are popular because they let a trader optimize his risk to any level he's comfortable with, as we will explain below. The more risk, of course, the more potential profit and also the more potential loss. But if you don't like risk, options also offer some extremely conservative strategies that will let you make a small amount of money with very little risk.

Options are traded using an option account, which is often another service offered by the same brokerage where you trade other securities. Most often, you will be required to keep a certain amount of money in your account.

Options Terminology

For some reason, the options market has a lot of odd-sounding terminology, with acronyms, and often multiple phrases that mean the same thing.

Strike Price - the price that was set on an option. This is the price at which the option holder can buy (for a call option) or sell (for a put option).

In the Money - this means that the current stock price is over the strike price for a call or under the strike price for a put option. In other words, this is the point at which the option holder can make a profit. Related terms with acronyms:

- In the Money (ITM) - the current price is better than the strike price.

- Out of the Money (OTM) - the current price is worse than the strike price.

- At the Money (ATM) - the current price and the strike price are about the same.

It's important to note that ITM and OTM do not necessarily indicate that an option is profitable, because there are some other factors to consider. These terms really just indicate the relationship between the current and strike prices.

The "Covered Call": A Conservative Strategy

The "covered call" is not a day-trading strategy, but it is a very useful technique for any trader and it illustrates a number of ideas about options that we will use later. In a covered call, you sell a call option, with a strike price that is higher than the current price, against a block of stock which you already own, and which you are thinking of selling anyway. This strategy is as conservative as any trade can be: you can almost certainly make a little money, with very little risk. Most likely, the worst that can happen is that you won't make as much money as you could have.

Here's how it works: let's say you already own 100 shares of Amalgamated Treeshade, which is currently selling for $100 a share. You're thinking of unloading this, but you don't have to make any immediate moves. So you go to the options market and sell a call with a strike price of $110 per share and a time limit of three months. In other words, you have sold some other trader the right to buy your shares for $110 each, anytime over the next three months. You sell this right for, let's say, 85 cents a share or $85 total.

The $85 dollars is yours to keep in any event. You can put that in your pocket and go out to spend it on a very nice dinner for two.

For the buyer, this call option is a pretty good deal. Three months is a long time, and the buyer knows that the price has been over $110 before, so it's a fairly good bet that sometime during the life of this option, the price is going to go above $110 per share. When that happens, the buyer will exercise his option and make you sell him that stock. Let's say the price has gone up to $115 per share. The buyer can turn around and sell that stock, and keep five dollars per share. He's just made $500, less the $85 he had to pay you for that option.

If you are a smart trader, you say "I feel good. I just sold my stock for $10 a share more than it was worth when I sold that option, so I made a thousand bucks, plus a dinner at a swell restaurant."

If you are a foolish and emotional trader, you smack yourself hard on the forehead and cry, "What a fool I was! If I hadn't sold that option, I could have sold that stock for $15 a share more, and made another five hundred dollars." If you're that kind of trader, (1) you will go broke fairly shortly, because you lack the emotional stability you need for trading, (2) you will be unhappy most of the time you're still trading, and (3) your forehead is going to hurt.

If the stock price never does go above $110, then when the option expires you still have your stock and you still have the $85 from the sale of the option. You can go out and sell another option against the same block of stock. The buyer of that option misses his $85 but isn't otherwise hurt.

But think about that time period of 3 months. When the option is fresh, three months gives plenty of time for the stock price to move, so that option is worth $85. As days pass, it becomes less and less likely that the option is going to go ITM (In The Money) in the remaining time. When it gets to the point that the option expires tomorrow, it's worth only a few pennies at best, because only an incurable optimist is going to believe the stock price will move ITM overnight.

Options are contracts which can be bought and sold like any other asset. As a covered-call investor, you don't care what the current value of your call option is because you've already gotten the money for it.

But if you are a day-trader in options, you may be interested in buying that call option or selling it to someone else. To make this point more strongly, there's almost no market for one-day puts and calls. A day trader in options is buying and selling options that still have some time before they expire.

Here's what you need to know about day-trading in options:

1. Time is Money. Options usually are worth most when they are fresh, and lose value steadily after that. But there are very profitable exceptions if the underlying value of the stock moves so that the option begins to look like a better bet.

2. A day trader rarely holds on to an option long enough to exercise it. Instead, you buy or sell options to other traders. At some point, either the option is worth exercising (this is said to have "intrinsic value") or it times-out and is worth nothing. An option that has intrinsic value may still be worth selling rather than cashing in – you might be able to sell it to someone who believes it will gain even more intrinsic value.

Is Options Trading for You?

Buying and selling options over a longer time horizon than a day offers a whole range of patterns from very conservative (such as the covered-call option described above) to very risky. As always, the more risk you take, the greater the potential reward and also the greater the potential loss.

Day-trading in options is a little different. It is a kind of trading you can do without much capital, and it offers the chance of very good returns. But it requires a tremendous study of various strategies and patterns, more than can be covered in this book, to account for all the factors that make options more or less valuable. These include:

- The time to expiry and the cost of the option.

- The relationship of the strike price to the current stock price.

- The particular prospects of the company whose stock is optioned.

- The mood of the market.

- Technical price-action patterns similar to those discussed above for stock trading.

If you are willing to invest the time and study, and to accept inevitable losses, then day-trading in options may be a money maker for you!

8. Day Trading on the Foreign Exchange Market

Everybody likes to have United States dollars, but they're not legal currency anywhere except in the United States. $US are theoretically not good anywhere else.

As a practical matter, though, people all over the world will sell you stuff for $US, because they have faith that they can sell those $US dollars to somebody who will pay for them in whatever local currency they actually do use.

The definition of "money" is anything at all that you can exchange for stuff or services. Anybody in another country who has $US believes that eventually those dollars will get back to America and be valuable to somebody who wants to buy something for them. In the meantime, they're valuable as money because the person who holds them can exchange them for stuff or services, wherever they are.

The market in the middle that allows people to exchange one currency for another is called Foreign Exchange or Forex.

The price of money goes up or down just like anything else that can be bought or sold. Here's an example with the fictitious country of "Elbonia" (with apologies the cartoonist Scott Adams). In Elbonia, the money is goats. If you're going to visit Elbonia (not recommended!), the Elbonian bank will exchange your $US in this ratio at, say, 9:00 AM on a particular morning:

You'll get 3.16 Elbonian Goats for each US dollar you have. (How can you have 0.16 of a Goat? The answer is too technical to present here. Trust us.)

However, that price changes every few minutes, depending on how many people want to exchange their money for Elbonian Goats. If there are lots of tourists coming to Elbonia (why?), the bank might find that by the afternoon, it only has to offer 2.86 Goats to get one dollar. To put this another way, there are a lot of dollars chasing the Elbonian currency, so each dollar is worth less in that exchange. This has no effect on the value of the $US in the United States, which continues to be what it always was.

On the other hand, if the truth about how Elbonian food tastes gets out to the tourists, they'll leave. The bank might have to offer 4.23 Goats per dollar in the afternoon. That is, the bank has to pay more in Goats to get a dollar.

That evening, you cash in your Goats for $US. If the price of dollars went up (a trader gets more Goats per dollar), then your Goats are not worth as much and you wind up with fewer $US than you had when you started. If the price of dollars went down (a trader gets fewer Goats for one dollar), then your Goats will be worth more dollars and you will have made some money.

The Foreign Exchange Market

The Foreign Exchange market (Forex) is completely decentralized. Unlike stocks, which are traded on only a few exchanges, the Forex market is known as an "over-the-counter" market and takes place all over the world. Much of it is inter-bank exchanges that nobody else ever sees. Moreover, because there are so many venues for exchanging currencies, there is typically not one exchange rate between two currencies, but a range of rates depending on where you make the exchange.

Forex runs 24 hours a day during the week, but is not active on weekends. It is the most liquid market there is. During the hours it is open, you can exchange any currency for any other at any time.

Currencies are always traded in pairs, such as $US and Euros, or Australian Dollars and Yuan (the currency of China). In each case, each currency has a price expressed in the other currency. An example might be EUR/USD (Euros to US Dollars) 1.3519 bid and 1.3525 ask. The **bid** price is what you will get if you sell either currency, and the **ask** price is what you will pay to buy that currency.

Note that your Forex broker does not charge a fee or commission for transactions. Instead, the broker gets its income from the **spread** between the bid and ask prices.

Profits and losses in Forex transactions are measured in **pips**, where a pip is 0.0001 of the value of a currency – in other words, one one-hundredth of one percent. (Exception: for the Japanese Yen, one pip is defined as 1%.) A **block** of currency is 100,000 single bills of that kind of money, and is the basic unit of Forex trading. (However, your broker will probably offer "mini" and "micro" blocks that will let you trade much smaller amounts.)

Example: Suppose you are trading Canadian Dollars against US Dollars and CAN/USD changes from 1.0345 to 1.0350. If you are holding Canadian Dollars, you can sell them for US Dollars and make 5 pips per Canadian Dollar. If you are trading one block, then your profit in US Dollars is:

100,000 X 0.0005 = 5. You just made 5 bucks American!

The value of a pip changes every moment, until you complete a transaction and buy or sell your block of currency.

Forex trading is almost always done on **margin**. You put a certain amount of money into your account with the broker, and the broker extends margin to you so that you can buy or sell much larger volumes of currency. Your broker will specify how much actual cash you need to put in to get started – as always, this must be money you can afford to lose. Note that if you lose money and your account runs dry, your ability to trade stops at that moment, even if you are in the middle of a transaction.

A Forex **robot** is a computer program you can run on some trading platforms that will execute trades for you. Naturally, every seller of robots will say their product is a guaranteed profit maker and just as naturally, you won't believe them. However, a robot chosen after diligent research (which means that you understand what the robot is doing and why) may be a good choice for you.

Why Exchange Rates Vary

What makes the Forex market volatile is that many, many factors affect currency exchange rates. These include the underlying strength of a country's economy, the available of credit for a country on the world market, the general state of the world economy and the export/import balance of a country.

In addition, currency trading is subject to the same kinds of news, rumors, and gossip that make all other financial markets wiggly.

All of this is to say, your constant study and attention will be necessary to prosper in this market.

Day Trading Forex

Despite being done on margin, day trading Forex can be a fairly safe and conservative activity. Most day traders follow strategies that are similar to those used for stock trading. In particular, Forex day traders often use the trend follower, scalping, and price action strategies.

If you are cautious about creating a rational trading strategy and sticking to it, without "bailing out" prematurely when you get nervous about losing money and without staying longer than your strategy suggests when you are winning, then you can make a good income day trading in the foreign exchange market.

Conclusion

I hope this book was able to help you to understand how day-trading works with various kinds of financial products, and how you can make a profit by trading.

The next step is to find an exchange that will let you set up a practice account, which will let you buy and sell with play money. Keep notes of what works and what doesn't as you practice trading. At the same time, study, study, study! Study more about how day-trading works, study about the companies whose stock you want to trade. Try to develop your own strategy for trading, and change it until you get something that works.

Then you can start trading with real money.

If you have enjoyed this book, please be sure to leave a review and a comment to let us know how we are doing so we can continue to bring you quality ebooks.

Thank you and good luck!

Book 2: Day Trading

A Comprehensive Guide to Making Money with Day Trading

Preface

This book is a comprehensive guide for new day traders. Day trading has been described as a "way of life" implying that the day trader must be completely absorbed in the activity, to the exclusion of everything else in life. That is not true. Successful day traders can work only a few days a week or only a few hours a day. Most day traders have profit as their motive and how many hours each week they spend studying the market and trading, the more money they can earn. Day traders are interested in all forms of investment; stocks, foreign currency exchange, exchange-traded funds and more. Profits can be made by well-informed and savvy traders in every one of these areas.

In this book, we will generally refer to trading in stocks, implying equities. This is only for simplicity for the readers. Almost everywhere, the information applies equally to all the other financial instruments, as well. There is also an important disclaimer we must state. Day trading in Equities, Futures, Currencies and Options has large potential rewards, but also large potential risk. You must be aware of the risks and be willing to accept them in order to invest in the equities, futures, currency and options markets. Do not trade with money you cannot afford to lose.

In terms of vocabulary, in this book, we use the short phrase "go long" for issuing buy orders and "go short" for issuing sell orders. Be aware that like with any other trading, you can sell instruments you don't own, by using a margin trading account.

This book is neither a solicitation nor an offer to Buy/Sell futures, stocks or options or any other financial instruments. No representation is being made that any account or trader will or is likely to achieve profits or losses similar to those discussed in this book. The past performance of any trading system or methodology is not necessarily indicative of future results. The author of this book does not hold a position in any of the stocks mentioned.

Chapter 1 Introduction to Day Trading

Make no mistake, day traders can make money in a matter of minutes, often in small amounts but on large number of stocks, those few cents can add up to large profits. However just as you can make a lot of money fast, you can also lose money at incredibly high speeds. Not every trade the day trader makes will result in profits. Sometimes it seems that the market is completely random, not following anything resembling logic or predictability. The market is volatile and fast. Prices can change at what seems like the speed of light. However, the market for any given stock follows some well-understood patterns. It is these patterns and their predictability that day traders use to their advantage. Stocks do not always follow these patterns and when they don't, traders can lose money. But when they do and the trader is positioned correctly, day traders can and do make a lot of money.

Only a small fraction of traders on all markets are day traders. Most of them are more conventional investors. And, not all investors use the same strategies because individual investors have different objectives. Some investors are looking for security; others are looking to take advantage of the yields from options. There are as many strategies as there are investors. Day traders also have their own strategies and objectives. We will look at some of these different types of investors.

Buy and Hold

Most investors buy stocks (or bonds or other financial instruments) with the idea of buying the instruments, and holding them for an extended period of time, collecting dividends for some stocks and capital appreciation for most. This is the source of revenue and income but it requires that at some time, they must sell the holding. Most investors rely on this buy and hold strategy for building portfolios and saving for the future. Investors must pay attention to the market but daily checking is usually not necessary. Looking over your portfolio once a month or so is usually fine to keep an eye on your positions. Over the long-term, buy and hold investors can build substantial portfolios, but it is not quick.

IRA's (Individual Retirement Accounts) usually operate as buy and hold accounts. Dividends can accumulate, and these investors can set up a DRIP (dividend reinvestment program) to continue accumulating positions automatically. To a great degree, investors like Warren Buffet use buy and hold along with DRIP to build value automatically.

Buy and hold investors use fundamental analysis to judge which instruments to buy or sell. They are concerned with the quality of the company, effectiveness of the management team, the products or services offered and how competitive they are in their industry. These investors look for quality of the product or service, favorable balance sheets, strong profit and loss statements and all the other indicators of fundamental quality.

Trading in Options

Options trading is a short-term action in which the investor buys or sells call or put contracts in some financial instrument. Options have an expiration date, and are either "in the money" or "out of the money" at expiration. The investor can sell positions, puts or calls, before expiration but frequently holds them until they expire. Puts and Calls are buy and sell contracts on blocks of stocks with a specified expiration date. Option contracts are valid until the expiration date and in some cases, are 'assigned' that is, required to be acted upon or else they expire with no value.

Options trading is very market-knowledge intensive and investors must train extensively to do so successfully. Like any other trading model, options trading is inherently risky and can result in major losses for the careless or inattentive investor.

Unlike buy and hold investors, options traders may be less concerned with fundamental analysis since they are only going to hold the option for a limited time. Options traders usually use a combination of fundamental and technical analysis, to determine their choices.

Like all investing, options trading is exciting and can be very profitable, but the investor must study and practice options trading before risking any real money. Options traders can lose money at an amazing rate if the trader is not alert and experienced.

Swing Trading

Swing traders buy and sell various stocks, futures, and currencies and hold them for only a few days, usually less than a week. They rely on keeping alert to the market and acting to open or close a position quickly, but not as fast as a day trader. Many of the same skills and knowledge are required for swing trading as for day trading.

Day Trading

So, how is Day Trading different? Unlike buy and hold investing and options trading, the day trader is almost always in and out of all positions by the end of the trading day. When the market closes, the day trader will have closed all her positions. This need to close out is because day trading is done "on margin," that is, the trader never owns the shares she is trading but, in effect, borrows them from the broker. Most brokers have a percentage fee for holding margin accounts and that margin fee will be imposed if the position is not closed out before the end of the trading day. Usually, brokers do not charge the margin fee for less than one day.

This means the day trader must be very alert to what is happening in the market during the trading day, to close positions that start to lose money or perhaps extend positions that are making money.

Day traders do not care about the underlying value of the stock or other instrument. They are concerned only with the volatility of the market, not the underlying values or the condition of the firm. In fact, under some circumstances, bad news for a company can translate into good news for day traders. Profits in day trades are made based on short-term variations, sometimes only minutes or hours in share prices.

An important feature day traders care about is liquidity. Liquidity means that there are many shares being traded, so when she makes a trade, shares are available for purchase and when she decides to sell, there are buyers who are interested. Penny stocks and shares with little volume are not good candidates for day traders because they probably lack both volatility and liquidity.

Another important fact about day trading is that it is a zero sum game. That is, for every winner, there is a loser. When a trader makes a profit, it has a corresponding loss for someone else. Buy and hold strategies and options are different. They are not zero sum games. Frequently, it is the day trader's broker who is the loser in a trade.

What can day traders buy and sell? The answer to that question is "Almost anything." The most popular instruments for day trading are equity stocks but that may be only because there are so many of them. An exception is the group called 'penny stocks." This exception is due mostly to the lack of volume being traded in penny stocks. Without trading volume, there may be few shares available for trading, both buying and selling. A day trader buying so-called penny stocks may not find a buyer when it comes time to sell them. Similarly, going short on a penny stocks risks not finding a seller when it is time to buy to close the position.

Day traders often trade in currencies through foreign currency exchanges (Forex). Day trading in Forex is a specialty that requires even more knowledge, experience and information. Forex day traders must keep up to date on all the currency exchanges since major moves in one, US dollars versus Euros, for example, may influence other currencies like the English Pound or the Australian dollar. Forex trading should be undertaken by only the most experienced day traders. We will not explore Forex trading in this book.

Futures contracts are similar to options contracts in the sense that they specify the details of a future buy or sell agreement for some quantity of a specific asset, at a specified price and on a specific date. They differ from options contracts in that the futures contract must be settled, either by delivery of the asset or in cash, on the specified date. Futures can be for commodities or financial instruments. Commodities can range from petroleum and corn to wheat or coal. Like Forex trading, commodities trading is a specialty, which can give the wise trader large profits or great losses. Forex and commodities trading is like handling a rattlesnake. It takes nerves of steel, enormous knowledge and skill but even the best can get seriously bitten.

Day traders may also specialize in trading options contracts. All of these are specialty areas that day traders can study, trade in and profit from. On the other hand, an unwary day trader can lose money at a remarkably fast rate. Risk is always high. There are stories about day traders who work from a lounge chair on the beach or at some faraway island paradise. Forget that. Day traders must be on the job nearly all the trading day or at least in a position to open or close positions on short notice. It is an exciting business but also one with a high level of stress. Any trader who lays awake at night worrying about his position may not be a good candidate for day trading. Some experts report that 90% of people who start day trading drop out after only a few months or a year. The success rate is very low and only the best 1% makes fortunes doing day trading. However, anyone who is enthusiastic and trains well can make a nice profit from day trading.

The key is to learn everything about day trading before you start and practice with a paper-trading platform, before using real money. There are no guarantees, at all.

There is an important lesson here. Wherever you are now, to move to where you want to be, requires effort on your part.

Make no mistake, even though day trading can be rewarding, it is risk involved. The best way day traders can ameliorate this risk is to know what they are doing. It requires planning your trades and then carrying out the plan.

It also requires confidence and a willingness to accept the risk without letting it affect your personal or financial health. A tough stomach is a good asset for a day trader.

Day trading is also more complicated than trading in individual shares as buy and hold or options. In a conventional stock trade for say, for instance by a buy and hold investor, you send an order to your broker, she forwards it to the market maker at the exchange, the market maker executes the trade and the trade is finished.

In day trading, it is a little more complex. Your order, as a day trader online, is issued through a day trading platform. Your platform may not include all shares in the market, so in some cases, the trader may need to subscribe to more than one platform service. Whichever platform includes the shares you want to trade, then sends your order to the broker. Usually the broker offers their own proprietary platform as a service to its clients. The broker then forwards the order to a clearinghouse, which deals with the market makers. If the market maker does not cover that particular share or, in the case of a short sell, does not have the shares available to lend, he will need to send the order to someone else that has those shares. The order then goes back to your broker, and you will be charged a fee for the search service. This is often a hidden cost to the day trader that will lower the profitability of the trade. New day traders need to examine this and other fees that they will be charged for various services.

Okay, so what determines the price of any share in the market? The individual share prices are determined by the very well established law of supply and demand. If more investors want to buy a particular share, the price will be bid up to where the people who hold those shares are willing to sell. There is a shortage of supply. If a particular share goes out of favor, investors no longer seek it out and are willing to sell shares at a price lower than what they might normally expect. Hence, the price goes down. The total market is made up of hundreds of thousands and sometimes millions of shares being demanded or sold, balancing supply and demand. This total market varies based on all these individual streams of trading and by external conditions, which can and do affect the general market.

These conditions may be economic or monetary changes in major sectors of the market, natural disasters like hurricanes, typhoons, earthquakes and many more events, which change the market as a whole. Thus the price of any particular share is affected by a myriad of internal and external influences. In reality, "the market" is the end result of a myriad of individual decisions made by millions of individual traders and investors, brokers, investment funds, insurance companies, banks and others. These decisions can be made, in these days of computer trading, thousands of times per second. They can be based on financial news, real hopes and fears, irrational hopes or fears, national news, reports from the Federal Reserve, and some of the market's movements are, frankly, just random, that is without a distinct explanation. Emotions play a large role in determining the direction and level of the market and any particular sector or stock. One thing all investors but particularly day traders must control is their own emotions and must recognize when other traders are reacting based on emotions.

Technical traders use the charts and reports provided by their platform to follow the prices of shares of interest by the minute, by the hour or by longer periods. A widely used chart is called a "candlestick" chart, which follows the share activity based on the selected time period. Technical traders who follow the wavy lines every day begin to see patterns in the way the line wiggles. Traders who see true patterns make money trading. Traders who jump to conclusions, or see false patterns, lose money. The technical analysis strategies in this book are some, but not all of those that traders have found to be usually true, and useful, over time.

Selecting a Trading Platform

Every day trader needs a trading platform, the set of software that allows the trader to examine the performance of stocks and the other instruments of interest to day traders, on a timely basis, because trades must be made quickly, accurately, and efficiently. The platform must provide a variety of stock analysis tools from which the trader can choose. There are some important features that must be available for a good platform and no trader can succeed without an adequate platform. Most brokers who engage in day trading offer their clients their own proprietary platform. The last section of this book lists a limited number of brokers and platforms, by no means exhaustive. As traders progress in their experience and knowledge, they often find it important to change their platform to one more complex or that has more important features. Some of these are provided free by the brokers. Others are available only by subscription and the subscription prices vary across the board. The cost for these subscription platforms must be considered in making trading decisions. It is not essential that any trader use only the broker's platform. If there is a platform available that meets your needs better, select it.

Indicator Choice

Traders need to be able choose from several different indicators and signal systems, displayed clearly and promptly, in a manner that facilitates decision-making. Later chapters discuss the various indicators and signals; you will soon develop your own list of favorite indicators and techniques. Remember, the job of the day trader is to recognize certain patterns, understand what they are telling you and take appropriate actions by buying or selling, that is going long or going short. Experience gained through practice and study will allow you to recognize these patterns and signals productively. During your study and practice, pay attention to which indicators are clear to you and which usually give you good results.

Understand Commissions and Costs; Per Trade or Per Share

Day trading is not free. You may be surprised and sometimes dismayed by the variety of expenses for trading commissions, platform subscriptions, margin costs and lots of others. Be sure to examine all of these when selecting a broker and a platform. For example, brokers usually offer a fixed commission that may range from $1.00 to $9.99 for each trade, but remember that a typical day trade involves two trades; either a buy followed by a sale or a sale followed by a buy. That means two commissions for each opportunity. This is usually advantageous if you are trading large numbers of shares, numbers in the thousands. Day traders soon find themselves trading in larger and larger lots as their account value increases.

On the other hand, if you are trading a smaller number of shares, the per trade commission may be cheaper. Typical per share rates are about $0.005 per share. Thus, if you are trading fewer than 2,000 shares, a per share commission is less expensive, in this example compared with a fixed price commission of $10.00. You can select the commission type for every trade. Most brokers offer a choice for the trading commission, but none of them are free. You can choose to pay the commission by trade or by share.

Commissions by trade are fixed, regardless of how many share you are trading, both buying and selling. This choice is better for trades for large numbers of shares. Some brokers offer discounts on commissions based on the number of trades you make per month.

Electronic communications through computer systems and the internet make day trading possible. There is a substantial cost to this infrastructure that must be paid by the users. Called ECN for Electronic Communications Network, ECN fees are often charged back to the traders as a direct cost. Some brokers may conceal these charges in one way or another but ultimately, the traders end up paying them. This is another cost of trading that must be considered in selecting a broker and a platform.

Chapter 2 Technical Analysis

As we pointed out earlier, day trading is based on Technical Analysis, contrasted with Fundamental Analysis. Buy and Hold investors are concerned with Fundamental Analysis. An investor looks for a company with a strong market, a good management team, quality products and a reliable history. Day traders do not care about the stock and its fundamentals. It doesn't matter if the company or shares are solid or not. Day traders need two things:

> Volatility: success in day trading requires that the stock price is moving, and the more the better. Any stock that is just going sideways in a consolidation phase is not of interest to the successful day trader. The stock must be moving up or down in a particular pattern. Day traders must learn these patterns so they are not just guessing where the stock price will go next. Guessing will cost you a lot of money

since there are probably some very wise day traders out there that you are competing against. If they are better at reading patterns than you, you will lose a lot of trades and a lot of money.

Liquidity: not only must the share price be moving, there must be sufficient volume being traded so there will be customers and sellers for whatever shares you want to trade. You may remember as kids, trading things with other kids, like cards or marbles. If no one wants what you have to trade, you will not make a trade. The same thing is true with day traders. If there is very little volume, there will likely not be many buyers or sellers to make a deal work. Without liquidity, any significant trade you make, either buy or sell, is likely to affect the share price itself and cause more volatility in the market. No trader wants to affect the share price in the middle of a trade.

Volatility

Every day, millions of shares are traded on the markets, whether they are shares of equities, foreign currencies, indexes, or any other instrument. These trading decisions are made by individual traders and investors, all with their own best interests in mind and based on their own research and outlook. These millions of trades influence share prices for individual stocks but it really is national and global news that affects the whole market. For example, a change in the price of oil can ripple down and out to many sectors in the market, for example the energy, chemicals, transportation sectors and others. However, unless it is a dramatic event such as major war or earthquake, the entire markets in all countries around the globe will not be significantly changed.

Individual stocks will reflect news and changes that are closely related to that particular share. For example, local events can and do affect currency values, so Forex shares will reflect that news. However, if the particular stock or shares that you are trading are widely exchanged, your trade will not materially affect the price of the stock. Thus the millions or at least hundreds of thousands of shares that are being traded in a complex stream of trades, any individual trade will not affect price in the market.

Especially for equities and to a lesser extent, Forex, changes in the industry in general may very well induce volatility in all related share prices. Day traders exploit this volatility for profit.

One technical indicator of volatility is the spread between the Bollinger Bands. Bollinger Bands will be discussed later but in general, when the upper and lower bands are far apart, it indicates high volatility. When they tend to converge or squeeze together, it indicates lower volatility and when the spread is narrow and the volume increases, it indicates a breakout, either to the high side or to the low side.

Liquidity

Liquidity is the complement to volatility. Liquidity means that there is sufficient volume being traded so that when the day trader makes a purchase or a sale, there is a corresponding buyer or seller in the market.

Pivot Points, Support and Resistance

These are other important indicators. Let's imagine a candlestick chart for Tenet Healthcare. This chart has the pivot point (P) along with the support levels (S1, S2) and resistance levels (R1, R2). Pivot points, support levels and resistance levels are mathematical calculations based on recent price performance which traders have found helpful for understanding the movement of prices. The pivot point on 1 minute, 5 minute, 10 minute and 15-minute charts are determined from the previous day's close using the following formula.

Pivot Point P = $\dfrac{(High + Low + Close)}{3}$ all from the previous day.

Pivot points reflect the most recent trading levels and are signals for coming shifts. A rule of thumb is that if the stock goes above the pivot point, it will probably end the day higher than yesterday. If it goes below the pivot point, it's probably headed down.

Resistance and support levels are calculated from the pivot point according to these formulas.

$$S1 = (P * 2) - High$$

$$S2 = (P * 2) - (High - Low)$$

$$R1 = (P * 2) - Low$$

$$R2 = P - (High - Low)$$

A **resistance level** (R1, R2) is a price that that a stock (or other instrument, such as an option or Forex block) doesn't seem to want to go above. Remember that trading on the market involves a lot of emotion. There are some price levels that traders regard as an appropriate level. When a stock starts trading above a resistance level or below a support level, we call that a 'breakout' and a significant event may have happened. This imaginary candlestick chart has the pivot point, support levels and resistance levels for prior periods, which is useful for watching changes over time. The prior period resistance and support points are shown as dotted blue lines. The pivot points are solid blue lines.

You can also approximate the resistance level for a stock by looking at this history over the past few months. If it has gotten up to, say, $26 several times but rarely goes above that, then $26 is a resistance level. For whatever reason, when the stock gets that expensive, investors think it's overpriced and they begin to sell it off. You can also describe the resistance level by drawing a line on the price chart that touches the recent highs.

Of course, this suggests your strategy: if the stock is close to hitting the resistance level, sell it short, because it will probably go down.

A **support level** is the opposite, a price that a stock doesn't seem to want to go below for pretty much the same psychological reason; a price that seems oversold and is a bargain. You can calculate support levels S1 and S2 by the formulas above or by looking at the charts for the last few months and observing the lows. Sometimes, support levels, like resistance levels can be approached several times before breaking through. Your strategy is to buy long at about that point, because the stock will probably go up. Of course, you don't have to do these calculations. Most charting services provide P, R1, R2, S1 and S2 automatically. Just let the computer do the work.

Resistance and support levels tend to occur at even-dollar values. The reason is that automatic buy and stop-loss orders are usually set for integer dollars. If a stock price gets down to, say, $31 and a lot of stop-loss orders kick in at that point, then a lot of stock will be for sale at $31 and it will be hard for the price to go lower.

Chapter 3 Trading Strategies and Signals

The most important part of any trade is determining an entry point and an exit point. Buy and Hold traders may keep a particular stock for years. Day traders hold stocks for minutes or hours. Planning is probably the most important component of successful day trading.

Planning starts with selecting a sector, such as consumer goods, retail stores, automotive industry, Forex, and so forth. Pick a sector you know something about; maybe one you have worked in or for which have a special interest. Think about this carefully. All of these sectors offer opportunities for day traders but each is different, has different leaders; some are cyclical like automotive, and each one responds differently to general economic conditions. Some, like consumer staples are fairly stable in down turns but have individual volatilities. The list of sectors is endless, but you are better off to limit yourself at the start.

Within your selected sector, pick one or two stocks with which to start. Concentrate on those stocks and learn everything you can about them; their position in the industry, profitability, volatility and liquidity. Study their recent candlestick charts and look for past patterns and signals and how the prices respond to those signals. Mentally back test them, to see what happened after a particular signal. We will learn a lot more about signals in this Chapter.

Here are some of the many important signals used by day traders. Some of them are very simple and others are more complex and need understanding to use them properly.

Candlestick Charts

Here are some important features of candlestick charts. The candlesticks show the level of opening and closing prices as well as the extremes during the period, which may be of any specified duration, one minute, five minutes, fifteen minutes and so forth. You can pick the interval on your platform. Thus the charts for different periods will have different appearances.

The candlestick is either red or green, depending upon the opening and closing prices. If the stock opens at a particular price and closes at a higher price, the candlestick will be green. Conversely, if the stock closes below the opening price, the candlestick will be red, indicating a drop during the period. The computer programs used to construct these charts can produce charts for all of the time periods selected. The 'wicks' above and below the candlestick show the highest and lowest prices during that same period.

These wicks indicate the variability during the

period, in both upward and downward directions. This is an indication of the volatility of the price during that period.

Indicators

Indicators are mathematical constructs, usually based on the stock data according to some well-known formulas and are sometimes called "Oscillators" because they move up and down depending on the shifts in prices. There are literally dozens of indicators that are used for various purposes. Depending upon the formula used, indicators may be called "Leading" or "Lagging", depending upon whether they are forward looking or backward looking.

Three important indicators are the MA, MACD and the RSI. MA is the moving average, frequently calculated for 200 days and 50 days. Naturally, the 50-day average better reflects recent changes in price where the 200-day moving average smoothes out more of the noise, to better represent the price history of the stock. We will discuss each of these indicators.

These are both indicators and overlays. Indicators are shown above or below the candlestick area; overlays are in the candlestick area as extra, usually colored lines. The dialog box at the top of the chart shows the conditions for the overlays, such as the Moving Average (MA) and the number of days in the average.

Plan Your Trades

Day traders also have to protect their positions. Before an experienced day trader makes a trade, the night before his next trading day, he examines the charts for the last trading day, examines the stocks in which he is interested and notes the signals and indicators. A smart day trader limits the number of stocks of interest for trading so he can examine them carefully to plan the next day's trades.

Stop Points

In doing so, he will plan the stock he chooses to trade, decides whether to go short or long and establishes entry and exit points. All of this is essential for success. If he is going to short a stock, his greatest concern is over an increase in the price during the day, so he sets a stop buy. For example, if he plans to sell short a particular stock at $25. He will set a stop point above that price, to protect himself against an increase in price. Without a stop loss, if his plan is faulty and the stock goes up instead of down, he must buy it back quickly at a higher price and accept the loss. The first resistance level is a possibility but entails the risk of volatility causing the buy order to kick in too soon, only to see the price drop dramatically. Experience is your best guide on setting stops.

Conversely, if he decides the stock price will rise, he must protect against a severe drop when he sets up his long position. If the price goes down drastically, he must sell before he loses too much money.

A savvy day trader sets three stops; one is a hard

stop or a trailing stop that represents the maximum loss the trader is willing to accept. The next is a mental stop, a point at which your entry criteria are violated. The market may have made an unexpected reversal and you don't want to get tangled in it. The other, the third stop is a daily stop. This is the point at which you conclude that today is not your day, and you close all positions and take the rest of the day off. Maybe you use it for more study or to take the kids to the beach.

Entry Points

If day traders had perfect future sight, there would be no need for predicting the change in price. However, we are humans and the market will often go against our plan. Entry points are just as important as stop loss points. The entry point is the price at which the trader intends to execute his plan. Most large movements in price take place during the first hour or so of trading. Many day traders will wait until the opening price is determined and allow a brief period for the 'noise' or jumps and falls to take place so the stock is more stable and can establish a steady trend, up or down. As soon as a trend is established, use caution in selecting entry and exit points.

1. When the trend line is clearly established, trade with that trend. If the trend is upward, assume a long position. If the trend is downward, plan to sell short. Remember intraday trends do not continue forever. They can reverse quickly and the day trader needs to be quick to respond.

2. Set profit goals. Remember, that you will

probably not make large profits, like several dollars on a given trade. Instead, set a profit goal, which may be as small as a few cents or larger, exactly how much depends on the volatility of the price. Day trades make money not on big killing trades but rather, on small gains on many shares of stock. For example, a gain of ten cents ($0.10) on ten thousand shares will yield a profit of $1,000. Not bad for a trade that may only last a few minutes. Set a goal for each trade, and **don't get greedy**. If you are long on a stock and it goes up $0.10, which you set as your goal, close your position and take your profit. If the stock continues upward, you can enter again and set a new profit goal. Make your plan and then carry it out. Exit when your goal is met and not before or after. Remember, emotion plays a large role in the market. Keep your emotions out of your trades. You will never lose money taking a profit.

3. Trade strong stocks on an uptrend and weak stocks on a downtrend. Many day traders compare various stocks against an index such as the Dow-Jones, S&P 500 or NASDAQ. If they strongly follow the index, when the index is up-trending, the strong stock may follow or even exceed the index. These are strong stocks and traders often go long on them, based on the trend in the index. If the index is in a downtrend, strong stocks may even buck the trend. On the other hand, weak stocks, those who do not follow the index, may be

candidates for short sales. Follow the usual rules for both these trades, by setting entry, exit and stop points.

Moving Average Crossover

An important and easy to understand signal is crossover of the moving average. Moving averages, whether exponential or arithmetic represent the average of closing prices for some specified period of time. Longer time periods when calculating moving averages, smooth out the "noise" or erratic nature of the data, giving a better sense of trend. Longer periods like 200 days, dampens out much of the noise and allows a good assessment of long-term trend. However, long averaging periods are not as responsive as shorter periods. Therefore, a very useful signal comes from comparing short-term average with longer-term average, giving a look at coming changes in trend. It thus is a leading indicator.

MACD Moving Average-Convergence/Divergence

MACD is the "Moving Average-Convergence/Divergence" and is a comparison of two moving averages, usually 26 days and 12 days with the 9-day moving average as a separate signal line.

In the MACD indicator, the exponential moving average or EMA is used rather than the arithmetic average. The exponential moving average gives much more weight to the recent price history. To calculate MACD, subtract the 26-day EMA from the 12-day EMA. Remember that the line plotted is the difference between the 12 and 26 day EMA's. The difference is plotted on the chart as a smooth line. The difference line is then compared with the 9 day EMA, called the signal line. The signal line represents the most recent data and comparing the signal line with the difference line indicates convergence when they are approaching each other and divergence when they are spreading apart.

RSI Relative Strength Index

Another important indicator is RSI, the Relative Strength Index. RSI measures the speed and size of price movements of a financial instrument. It may be thought of as a first derivative of the price change over time as expressed in calculus mathematics. Like other indicators RSI is an oscillator and it has a mathematical range of zero to 100. It is generally accepted that RSI values over 70 indicate the share is overbought and an RSI of less than 30 is regarded as an oversold condition. However, it is a leading indicator, unlike MACD. RSI is an excellent measure of MOMENTUM, a concept every day trader needs to understand. Momentum can be thought of as the Emotion of the Market, the driving force behind price moves. It is the pressure, up or down, on the price, whether many traders are buying or selling. RSI is a leading indicator since it will rise or fall, albeit slowly sometimes, in advance of a price move. That is, there is still some energy left in the thrust, even though RSI is changing. If the momentum slows on an upward trend, the price will peak and start dropping, sometimes rapidly in response to a change in market sentiment.

RSI was developed by J. Welles Wilder in the 1970's, whose famous quotation should be on the wall over the desk of every day trader.

> **"Letting your emotions override your plan or system is the biggest cause of failure."**
> **J. Welles Wilder**

The RSI should not be used by itself for buy and sell decisions. Sometimes a stock can remain overbought for an extended period and conversely, can maintain an oversold condition for long periods. The clue as to whether the price will move is found in the volume being sold. When a stock is overbought and the volume is not great, most holders are waiting for other news. When an overbought stock suddenly sees a large volume being traded, it may indicate holders are taking profits and the price may decline in response to the supply/demand imbalance. The same logic is true for oversold conditions. When a large jump in volume takes place in an oversold reading, buyers are anticipating an increase. Thus, large volume changes in overbought RSI indicators may signal selling and it is time to be in a short position. Similarly, when volume jumps in an oversold reading, the price may increase sharply so that is a signal for the day trader to go long.

Bollinger Bands

The Bollinger Band indicator was developed by John Bollinger in the 1980's. The Bollinger Band indicator uses a moving average of recent prices for a specified interval and develops the +/- 1 or +/- 2 standard deviations to examine the "normality" of the price behavior. Standard deviation is a very commonly used statistic in many fields like engineering and quality control but also in finance and weather forecasting. The +/- 2 standard deviation includes 95% of the data. Any time the system exceeds or falls below the 2 standard deviation band, it indicates a significant change 95% of the time. Any occasion outside of either of the bands is an indicator of an overbought or oversold condition. In addition, when the bands converge, that is approach each other, it indicates a period of consolidation. A coming breakout is indicated by the convergence or contraction of the bands. Bollinger Bands are an excellent and widely used leading indicator.

Pay attention also to occasions when the price goes outside the upper or lower Bollinger Band. When that happens, a significant change is happening and the good day trader will be prepared to move. As a general rule, when a stock price exceeds the upper band, expect a pullback. Conversely when the price goes outside the lower limit, expect momentum to develop as many traders will be attracted to the bargain prices, volume will increase and the price will be bid up, sometimes very quickly.

Harami Pattern

The Harami pattern is often an indicator of a coming reversal. The Harami consists of a long candlestick followed by a short candlestick of the opposite color, completely within the previous candlestick. Harami patterns are a useful addition to all the other indicators a day trader uses. Let's imagine a case with the large candlestick being red, showing that the stock opened higher than it closed. That is followed by several green candlesticks that are within the limits of the first one. A day trader can expect an upward movement from this pattern and therefore it is called a bullish Harami. Let's also imagine that the second group is a green candlestick followed by a red Harami. This is a bearish pattern and the trader can expect a decline in the next period. Haramis are indicators that the buyers are very conservative, not taking the trading range outside of the previous range but switching the opening and closing sequence and hence the color reversal.

Doji

A variation of the Harami is called the doji. A doji occurs when the open and close are very close to the same, but different from the period high or low. In the case of a doji, the price may have opened at level, say 25, rose to a higher level, say 26, dropped to 24 but at the close of the market, returns to 25 or very close to 25. In the Harami exhibit, notice the several occasions when the open and close were very close to the same. These are called dojis and they indicate market uncertainty. Traders know something is going to happen but they may not know which direction it will go. In examining trends, dojis are frequently seen at the top of an uptrend, followed by a downtrend or at the bottom of a downtrend, followed by an uptrend. They are signaling that the market is about to change.

On Balance Volume (OBV)

On balance volume is a cumulative indicator, by adding the volume when a share closes higher than it opened (green candle), and by subtracting volume when today's close is below yesterday's (red candle). It measures the balance between buying pressure and selling pressure. It is a leading indicator and when used in conjunction with other indicators can lead to an accurate sense of a coming increase or decrease.

On Balance Volume should be available on your trading platform. It is an excellent momentum indicator, measuring the psychology of the market, sensing the level of interest, either increasing or decreasing. In practice, when investors gain interest in a particular stock, they will start buying (or selling) but the price does respond immediately. After the interest is observed by other investors, they may start bidding the price up or down. This momentum then is a leading indicator. OBV was developed by Joseph Granville in the 1960's and it has become an important leading indicator. It is computed by adding today's volume to yesterday's volume if it is larger but by subtracting today's from yesterday if it is lower.

Day trading platforms generally offer OBV as an indicator and display it as part of the candlestick chart.

Chapter 4 Case Study of Sonny Elias

We will look at some cases of new day traders and see how they can go about getting started. Naturally, these are not the real names of the people described.

Sonny Elias is a graduate of a Midwestern state university with a Bachelor's Degree in Business Administration and a minor in Marketing. He is now working for a nationally known insurance company as a licensed agent. He is licensed to sell Life and Health insurance as well as Liability and Casualty policies. He has been an insurance agent for about ten years and has a large 'book' of clients. Many of his new sales come from referrals by his current policyholders.

Most of his appointments are in the evenings and sometimes on weekends, to meet with clients and prospective buyers. All of his correspondence with the insurance company takes place over the telephone and internet and apart from the quarterly sales meetings, his schedule is completely flexible. He has an office in his home with high-speed internet access and facilities to meet with clients, although many of his appointments take place in the homes of clients and prospects.

Sonny wants to expand his scope and income. He is saving money regularly and has a good foundation in the stock market, worth about $130,000. He owns his own home and has a mortgage payment of $900 per month. He spends most of his days in his home office, making telephone calls, dealing with customer claims and occasionally meeting with clients. He has available cash sufficient to cover three months of expenses, his emergency fund.

Sonny is engaged to be married next year and although his current income is very satisfactory, he would like to explore new sources of revenue. He has been trading not just in stocks but also options and mutual funds. He feels like he needs to move forward and has interest in day trading.

What does Sonny need to do in order to get into Day Trading? First off, he needs to understand what Day Trading is and what it is not. How is Day Trading different from other trading models?

Here are some questions he needs to investigate. What is day trading? Day Trading is far different from regular investing. Some writers refer to Day Trading as a "Life Style" since it can become a full time occupation for the maximum gain but it requires a lot of attention during the trading day. Remember, when a day trader takes a position on a stock, he will close that position before the close of the market to reduce the risk of off-hours trading and losses as well as the overnight margin charges.

Sonny has decided to take $20,000 from his stock portfolio and use that as his account for day trading. When he contacted a day trading broker, they advised him of the Securities and Exchange Commission (SEC) rule called the Pattern Day Trader (PDT) rule that states a day trader's account must be a capitalized with a minimum of $25,000. This rule applies to US citizens and US based traders. He will need to capitalize his account for at least that amount. Otherwise, he will be limited to only three trades in any 5-day period. According to some writers, this is to keep people from starting with a small account and losing it quickly. Protecting the trader from himself, I guess.

The broker's representative also advised him to take advantage of their "paper trading account" which is similar to the simulators offered by some options brokers. This allows the new trader to get near-actual experience without risking his or her own real money. We strongly advise that every new day trader take advantage of this facility, to avoid beginner's mistakes. There is nothing that will discourage a new trader faster than taking losses on his or her first few trades. That will make the new trader just throw up their hands and abandon the whole idea, a little bit or very much poorer for the experience.

So, Sonny has decided to find a broker that offers paper trading as part of their service. Many brokers offer this opportunity as well as a technique called "back testing". Back testing gives the trader a chance to test various strategies based on historical data. The trader enters a strategy for a particular stock at a specified period of time and the simulator then reproduces the historical results allowing the trader to evaluate his strategy.

If the outcomes are not to his liking, he can adjust the strategy and see the new results. This is a very important training exercise. All new traders need to practice trades fully until they are well versed in the strategies and get consistently good results. This does not mean that all trades will be successful. Far from it. Most trades yield small profits and some losses, but by making enough well planned trades, the trader can make a fair amount of money.

In our case, Sonny has done extensive paper trading, studied technical analysis, learned several typical patterns and now feels he is ready to take the plunge with his own money. Sonny is looking at the automotive sector, which appears to be strong. There has been a recent economic recovery and all indications show it will continue for a while. However, remember that day traders are not concerned with general trends. They are looking at volatility and short term trends.

Sonny is interested in the automotive sector of the stock market. He begins by investigating Fiat Chrysler (FCAU). The first thing he should notice is that FCAU has been on an almost unbroken climb since the middle of October and has made substantial gains. The resistance levels have been exceeded consistently, including R2 on several occasions and is currently over R2. Another important indicator that is shown on a chart he is looking at is the "On Balance Volume." The

OBV has been increasing and slightly leading the price but it appears that the rate of gain in OBV is dropping slightly, perhaps predicting a downturn.

Let's now imagine that he is looking at a chart that is showing a tapering off of OBV, the price has turned down rather sharply. Observe also the other important indicators like RSI. RSI showed FCAU to be seriously overbought just before the downturn. MACD also dropped and crossed the signal line, and total volume has dropped significantly. Notice also that in the days just before the downturn, the price exceeded the upper Bollinger Band, indicating a non-normal event was occurring.

If Sonny had chosen to act on FCAU in early January, he would have been sensitive to the overbought condition and predicted a downturn. Acting on that knowledge, Sonny might have sold FCAU short and profited from the sharp downturn. To do this, he could have entered a short sale order for FCAU for 500 shares, at about 10.50, followed the drop down to about 9.25 and gained the difference. Of course, he also entered a stop at 11.00 to protect against an increase in price instead of a drop, and a buy order at his profit target of 9.25, giving him a 12% gain within a short period of time, of perhaps only a few hours.

Another important stock in this sector of course, is General Motors (GM). This chart that he is looking at has several instances of crossover for the 5-day and 15-day moving averages. In each case, the price rebounded rather quickly. There are also days when the price hit or came close to the Bollinger bands, both upper and lower. In early January, the 5-day MA broke downward. At this occasion, Sonny sold GM short at 37.50 and held it for a few hours, selling at 36.50. In this short sale trade, he made $1.00 per share for a total of 500 shares, netting him $500, less his commissions and fees. The signal for this trade was also the drop in on-balance volume (OBV), showing a weakening of the momentum.

Volkswagen (VLKAY) is another major player in the automotive sector. Here, Sonny was keeping track of the 3-day versus 20-day moving averages and the OBV. On January 9, he saw a jump in on balance volume and a continuing steep climb in the 3-day MA, departing sharply from the 20 day MA. On January 9, he went long for 500 shares of VLKAY at 31. He closed that day at about 31.50, gaining $250 profit. But as he watched the OBV continue to climb, the following day, he repeated the long position for 500 shares at 31.25 and closed at 31.50. This was not as large a gain but the following day, seeing the same signals, he again went long at 31.50 and closed at 32.25, for a gain of 0.75 per share or $375. During this short period, he collected a total profit of $750.

Another important automotive sector firm is Geely Holding (GELFY). Geely manufactures automobiles in China and London Taxis in Coventry, England. They also own Volvo cars and seem to be planning a separate stock offering for Volvo. They distribute Geely cars worldwide and are very successful in many markets, as well as in China. Sonny is now relying on several indicators, Bollinger bands, RSI, 3 day/20 day MA and OBV. In mid-December share prices hit the lower BB, indicating an unusual condition, RSI was strong, the 3 day **MA** line was climbing toward the 20-day line and on balance volume was solid and showing a gradual climb. This told him that **GELY** was about to increase and maybe rapidly. Because the stock price is very low, in the neighborhood of $1.00, he was able to go long on 2000 shares at 0.88.

Over the next several trading hours, **GELYF** rose to 1.10 where he closed, for a gain of $440. Because it has now hit the upper **BB**, he is watching closely for a pullback, which he can position for a short sale and another gain.

Sonny now has now gained confidence in his ability to recognize patterns. He is satisfied with his successes, although he has also had a few down days, but he is learning quickly and intends to continue day trading.

Chapter 5 Maryellen Curtis Case

Maryellen Curtis is a registered nurse. She is in her mid-thirties, divorced and has no children. She is not particularly interested in worrying about her retirement but she would like to build a cash position so she can travel on vacations and long weekends. She has an excellent salary but her job as a head nurse is stressful. Generally she works on the night shift, because she has found that night shift work seems to give her more time for herself.

To build the cash reserves she wants, she has turned to day trading. Her work hours lend themselves to giving her time to study and follow the market. Her friend, Martha has been day trading for several months and although she has had some losses, her profits are now starting to grow.

Maryellen is planning to use some cash that she inherited to start her day trading account. She is aware that in order to trade frequently, she must capitalize her account with at least $25,000, in order to meet the SEC requirements. She has inherited about $30,000 and plans to use it to start her new effort.

Maryellen has an emergency fund that will cover at least three months of living expenses of housing, food, insurance, and regular living costs, so she is ready and eager to get started.

Because of Martha's early losses, Maryellen has taken her education and training seriously. She started by studying with on-line training resources and reading everything she can about day trading. Because of her profession, she is particularly interested in the healthcare industry, hospital companies, pharmaceuticals and the like. It is always good to concentrate on a sector in which you have knowledge and familiarity. However, Maryellen tends to be a conservative trader, looking for clear signals rather than making spur of the moment decisions. For a buy and hold investor, several of the stocks she is looking at offer good opportunities but day traders must look for volatility and liquidity, with fairly clear signals.

After preparing by study and practice with paper trading, she looks for related equities. She knows that the same principles apply to patterns in all sectors, whether ETF's, equity stocks, or currency exchanges. One of the most important tools is the candlestick chart. Usually, web sites that supply charts will allow you to select the chart type and the candlestick chart is one of the most commonly used.

One of the first equities she looked at was Becton-Dickinson (BDX), a well-known manufacturer of medical devices including syringes for drawing blood and giving injections. Maryellen of course, has used many Becton-Dickinson products.

The volume jumped sharply and the candlesticks were green for five of the next six days. Alert day traders probably made fortunes in that six-day period. RSI took a sharp decline just ahead of that upward spike in both volume and price. A similar shift took place in the middle of November signaled by both volume and RSI another opportunity for an alert day trader.

Maryellen participated in both opportunities, in the first (August) by going long on August 6 with a purchase of 100 shares of BDX at 168 and riding it up to 169.00 by the end of the day, netting a profit of $100 by the close of trading that day. She repeated that long position the next day by buying at 170 and selling at close at 171, netting another $100. In all of these trades, when she made her plan, she also determined stop-loss and profit points, to protect her position. Sometimes, if the volatility is really high, a position will close out before reaching the profit point. These can result in loss of the commissions and fees but are good insurance.

Again in August, following the BDX chart she looked at, she went long for another 150 shares at $168 and closed at the end of the day at $170.50, gaining another $375.

In early November, when Maryellen noticed the

drop in RSI to around 30 indicating an oversold condition, she again went long on BDX, buying 150 shares at 170 and riding it up to 171 before closing out for the day for a gain of $100.

By the end of November, she had profited from BDX to the tune of some $575.00. Of course, she had some losing trades during the same period but by the middle of November, she had gained a lot of confidence in her ability in technical analysis. At the same time, she was closely following the news about BDX and realized really great profits from her day trading.

She also learned that she did not need to trade every day. She followed the market every day and kept up to date on the sector news but she needed only a few hours every day to watch the market and make her trading decisions.

In keeping with Wilder's advice, she made her trading plan and stuck with it, avoiding complicating her day trading success with her emotions. She also noticed that following the early November run-up, the RSI nearly hit 70, indicating an overbought condition and she could have earned more by shorting BDX during that steep drop from over 178 down to a low close to 162. Proper application of day trading principles during this period could have added considerably to her trading success. In this case, because of the extended run-up in early November, she should have noticed the corresponding increase in RSI and in this case, she could have shorted BDX and cashed in on the downturn. In this case, the old saying that anything that goes up must come down, and BDX did.

Another stock Maryellen is interested in is Johnson and Johnson (JNJ). With JNJ she began using another indicator, Bollinger Bands.

Among the pharmaceutical stocks, Johnson and Johnson is always interesting for traders interested in the healthcare sector. She notices how the volume surges in mid-August and again in mid-November presaged major price moves. From mid-August on until mid-September, the OBV indicated selling pressure, also shown by the contraction of the Bollinger Bands, shown in green. These were good indicators of significant price movement, an opportunity for alert day traders.

On November 10, she noticed the jump in volume traded, but with little change between opening and closing prices. This is typical of a doji, signaling uncertainty in the market and foreshadowing a possible downward break. On the following trading day, she shorted JNJ at 119 and watched the drop to about 118, netting $1.00 per share for her 200 shares for a profit of $200. She recognized that the share price closed still above the upper Bollinger Band, she shorted JNJ again the next day and gained $1.75 at her planned profit point for a gain of $350.00. JNJ continued to retract for several more days, affording more short sale opportunities, until it had dropped to a point close to the lower Bollinger Band. By now, Maryellen had really become sensitive to the Bollinger Bands and OBV as good indicators or price movements.

Notice that when a day trader is shorting a

particular stock, it does not mean a lack of confidence in the equity itself. Rather, since day traders depend upon volatility and liquidity, they do not even consider the underlying fundamentals. They rely only on price movements and the ability, through liquidity, to get into and out of a stock at an appropriate time. Day traders do not become cheerleaders for any stock.

Another stock of interest to Maryellen is Hospital Corporation of America (HCA). Like Tenet, HCA operates many hospitals across the country. She is looking at a chart showing almost the full year of 2016.

In mid-October, HCA saw a major increase, running from about 75 to about 82, over a short period of time. During that time, she notices the overbought condition indicated by RSI. MACD also indicates the dramatic upswing, indicated by the moving average being significantly higher than the 9-day signal line. In addition, the Bollinger Band spread increased during the period of increasing price. That increase was followed by a drop in the last half of October, signaled by a drop in RSI and moderate volume. However, after early November, the Bollinger band width decreased, indication a contraction followed by a jump in volume. That foretold the breakout which followed immediately. In mid to late December, HCA entered a period of consolidation, with low Bollinger Band gap and the candlestick showing a sideways movement. Had Maryellen detected the oversold condition of RSI and gone long with HCA at about 69 and let it ride up to 72 before closing out, she could have collected some $3 per share. That would have been a wonderful profit opportunity. The day trader must be alert to these indicators and be prepared to move quickly. Maryellen was now following the gap width on the Bollinger Bands shown at the bottom of the graph.

She also notices that the shares of HCA dropped dramatically immediately after, from about 80 to about 70 per share. If Maryellen had been long at that time, she would have suffered a big potential loss. She also observed that in spite of a sharp drop, the candlestick chart did not go red. That is a characteristic of the candlestick chart, when overnight, a stock price drops, opens at a lower price than the prior day, but closed higher than it opened, therefore the candle was green. A day trader could have gone short at the high point of the MACD in October and profited from the drop. The Bollinger Bandwidth also contracted during that decline, another signal of a shift in price.

Medtronic (MDT) is another interesting stock in the healthcare field. Medtronic is a leading producer of medical devices used by vascular and cardiac surgeons including pacemakers, and other implantable devices. Medtronic's earnings have been consistent although not spectacular, but ahead of its competitors. Headquartered in Dublin, Ireland Medtronic is a global firm with sales in essentially all markets. It appeared to be solid and stable until the On Balance Volume (OBV) suddenly swung toward indicating selling pressure in late November. She also notices a jump in volume and a squeeze in the Bollinger Bands at that time. This predicted a drop in price and sure enough, it went down by about $10 per share. Remember that jumps in volume precede major shifts in price performance. The drop in mid-November was a good opportunity to sell short, taking advantage of the coming slump. There were no changes in MDT's fundamentals at that point but recall that day traders do not look at fundamentals. This drop for Medtronic, Inc. may have been a consequence of market psychology. Successful day traders take advantage of market psychology to profit, day by day. MDT now appears to be in a consolidation phase, so Maryellen will wait to see here it goes from here. The contraction of the Bollinger Bands indicates a price performance shift is coming, but it does not indicate the direction. At this point, OBV shows heavy selling pressure which is supported by the RSI indicator, showing a strong oversold condition, which suggests that the shift will go to the high side, calling for a long position when the break occurs. The current price is also approaching the S1 support level, also suggesting a buying streak may take place.

As predicted by the several indicators, MDT saw a jump in price in early January, Maryellen took advantage of this prediction and went long with MDT early in January and collected several hundred dollars in profits. Success in day trading depends on the trader's ability to read the signs and signals.

Maryellen also looked at Abbot Laboratories (ABT). Abbot is a global manufacturer of a wide range of medical related products varying from pharmaceuticals to medications and glucose monitoring systems. They are an old company, founded in 1888 and headquartered in Abbot Park, Illinois. ABT has dropped from about $45 in August to around $38 in December. ABT is highly diversified and at the moment the RSI is about 46, showing no particular pressure for selling or buying. Although there may be opportunities for small gains day to day, at this point, the signs are that a price movement is likely coming. Maryellen likes the company, which shows both volatility and liquidity. Consequently, she has put this stock on her watch list and she will follow it into the next quarter, looking for clearer signals. Like what happened to Medtronic, ABT is likely to breakout to the high side in the very near future. A day trader's watch list is vital and he or she must keep looking at it for opportunities.

Chapter 6 Laura Dahl Case

Our next day trader example is Laura Dahl. She is married and has two children, both of whom are in school all day. Her husband is a good provider but she is interested in earning money to save for the children's college expenses. She has a number of years to accomplish this objective but she wants to try day trading. She has been actively trading options so she is not exactly a newcomer. However, she knows that day trading is different; more stressful, requires close attention and has its own language and requirements. She will do her day trading with her online broker, since they have a good platform for day traders and reasonably low commissions. She has some $50,000 in her brokerage account so she will use $40,000 of it for her day trading account. She plans to continue options trading and add day trading to her activities. Her broker also has excellent training facilities for new day traders and so she has taken advantage of that. She has carried out several weeks of 'paper trading' through her broker's platform and has satisfied herself that she can start day trading with real money.

Laura is interested in high technology and computer systems, as well as social media and health care. She is very familiar with modern technology and is excited about it. The first stock she wants to look at is Hewlett-Packard Enterprises, (HPE). HP is a widely recognized maker of electronics and electronic systems. HP underwent restructuring in 2015 to split into two operating entities, HP, Inc and HP Enterprises. HP, Inc handles the computer and printer business and HPE retains the technology.

Several features are important in the chart for HPE that she is looking at. The share price has increased from about $22 up to about $23 in December and overall has jumped from about $12 at the beginning of the year up to December's level of $24. At year-end, the MACD is below the signal level, OBV is steady, share price is at the Pivot Point and volume has been holding steady. It may be that a reversal is about to happen.

She notices that on the HPE chart, in early December, there was a strong upward movement forming the first part of an Harami, followed by several red candles, reversing the previous upward trend. On the first trading day of the New Year, HPE moved ahead and is now about the pivot point. All the other indicators seem favorable to Laura, so she decides to go long on HPE with 1,000 shares at $23.50. She is a little reluctant to commit too much since this is her first-day trade. At the end of the trading day, HPE had advanced to $23.75, so she took her gain and sold the

1,000 shares at $23.75 for a profit of $250. She is very satisfied with her first trade as a day trader.

Two other interesting stocks in the advanced microelectronics sector are AMD and NVDA. Advanced Micro Devices (AMD) is a producer of various chips and electronic devices, especially for graphics processing. Nvidia (NVDA) is a similar but somewhat smaller competitor in that field. Both are highly respected and offer both volatility and liquidity.

These stocks are showing different signals. AMD is currently bouncing around the lower Bollinger Band and the RSI is below the median of 50. The 5-day MA is well below the 15-day MA line, having crossed over in early January. This means momentum is lagging.

On balance volume had been strong until about the time of the crossover and has been slightly declining. At this time, AMD will be placed on Laura's watch list, while she watches for a bounce up from the lower BB line. She will watch for volume increases to trigger a new position on AMD.

Nvidia (NVDA) is interesting also. It sits presently at about the middle of the Bollinger Band range, RSI is over 55, indicating strength but the OBV has dropped recently from its previous high momentum reading. Volume for NVDA is much lower, at about 10 million shares daily compared with AMD, which is closer to 40 million. Both of them had been in an overbought condition in mid to late December but have backed off from that in January.

NVDA will also be put on Laura's watch list,

anticipating a movement, likely upward. She noticed that the Bollinger Bands have converged slightly, heralding a potential change.

Microchip Technology (MCHP) is another maker of these devices. In mid-January, she bought MCHP at 64 and saw it rise to 65.50, netting $1.50 for her 400 shares. At closing, she continued to be bullish on MCHP and went long again for 400 shares at 65 and saw that rise to 66 which was her planned profit point. This yielded an even $1,000 for the two days. Naturally, she had stop loss orders in place in case the price dropped.

She did not take a position the next couple of days but observed that the price had reached the upper BB and was followed by a green Doji. She took this as a signal for a reversal and prepared to short MCHP the next day. It is vital for day traders to examine the charts they are following every day, whether they plan to trade that day or not. Most traders wait until the market has closed and the charts have been updated, to plan for the following day's trades. This is another argument for following a limited number of charts, so you can concentrate on a few rather than trying to study many less closely.

Chapter 7 Partial List of Day Trading Brokers

These services are listed in no particular order and no recommendation is implied or should be inferred. These are websites of brokers who offer day trading services. Some brokers may have particular specialties such as futures or Forex whereas other may be more general. Most of them also offer brokerage services for buy and sell contracts and trades.

Each of them offers different trading platforms, mostly proprietary software and very different commission schedules. When new traders are looking for a broker, they should look carefully at the capabilities of the platform and the commission structure and other fees and charges. When actively trading large numbers of shares at very narrow spreads, fees and commissions can make an otherwise profitable trade into a loss. For very active day traders, many offer discounts based on the number of trades made per month.

Thinkorswim by TD Ameritrade

Lightspeed Trading

Advantage Futures

OptionsXpress

Trade Station

Options House by E*trade

Oanda

Ninjatrader

SpeedTrader

Scottrade

Interactive Brokers

Other websites offer free or subscription training and other services. Some of those are:

Stockcharts.com

Technitrader.com

Investopedia.com

Conclusion

I hope this book was able to help you to understand the basics of day trading. The next step is to begin research, study and practice with 'paper money' until you can gain insight and confidence in your day trading skills. Remember to continue studying and learning. That is the only way to get to your goal, of "where you want to be." And remember, plan your trade and trade your plan. Keep your emotions out of your trading business.

If you have enjoyed this book, please be sure to leave a review and a comment to let us know how we are doing so we can continue to bring you quality books.

Thank you and good luck!

Check out another book by Baron McBane

www.ingramcontent.com/pod-product-compliance
Lightning Source LLC
Chambersburg PA
CBHW070041210526
45170CB00012B/557